DATE DUE

Oct 7, 2008	

PRINTED IN U.S.A.

KOREA

The High and Beautiful Peninsula

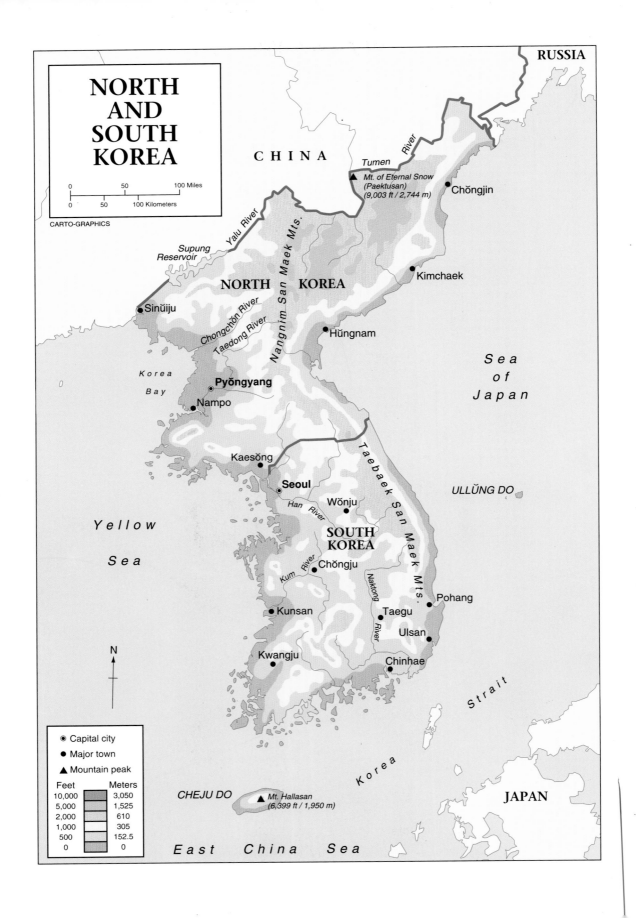

NORTH AND SOUTH KOREA

0   50   100 Miles

0   50   100 Kilometers

CARTO-GRAPHICS

RUSSIA

CHINA

Tumen   *River*

▲ Mt. of Eternal Snow
(Paektusan)
(9,003 ft / 2,744 m)

Chŏngjin

Yalu River

Kimchaek

*Supung
Reservoir*

NORTH   KOREA

Sinŭiju

Chongch'ŏn River

Taedong River

Nangnim San Maek Mts.

Hŭngnam

*Korea
Bay*

Pyŏngyang

Nampo

*Sea
of
Japan*

Kaesŏng

Seoul

ULLŬNG DO

Han   *River*

Wŏnju

Taebaek San Maek Mts.

*Yellow
Sea*

SOUTH
KOREA

Chŏngju

Kum   *River*

Naktong

Pohang

River

Kunsan

Taegu

Ulsan

Kwangju

Chinhae

N

Strait

● Capital city

● Major town

▲ Mountain peak

Feet	Meters
10,000	3,050
5,000	1,525
2,000	610
1,000	305
500	152.5
0	0

Korea

CHEJU DO

▲ Mt. Hallasan
(6,399 ft / 1,950 m)

JAPAN

East China Sea

EXPLORING CULTURES OF THE WORLD

KOREA

The High and Beautiful Peninsula

Dean W. Collinwood

BENCHMARK BOOKS

MARSHALL CAVENDISH
NEW YORK

*The publisher would like to thank Ben Hughes,
of the Korea Institute at Harvard University,
for his expert review of the manuscript.
The author wishes to thank John Park and Aaron
Brough for help with the research for this book.*

TO KATHLEEN AND THE CHILDREN

Benchmark Books
Marshall Cavendish Corporation
99 White Plains Road
Tarrytown, New York 10591-9001

© Marshall Cavendish Corporation 1997

Library of Congress Cataloging-in-Publication Data
Collinwood, Dean Walter, date
    Korea : the high and beautiful peninsula / by Dean W. Collinwood.
        p.   cm. — (Exploring cultures of the world)
    Includes bibliographical references.
    Summary: Discusses the history, geography, daily life, and culture of the Asian nation
on the peninsula between China and Japan.
    ISBN 0-7614-0337-x (lib. bdg.)
    1. Korea—Civilization—Juvenile literature.   [1. Korea.]   I. Title. II. Series.
DS904.C65   1997
947' .71—dc20   96-20602
                                                                 CIP
                                                                  AC

Printed in Hong Kong
Series design by Carol Matsuyama

Front cover: Korean women in bright, traditional dress.
Back cover: A group of Korean children pose for a picture.

Photo Credits
Front cover and pages 26, 27, 39, 49: ©Steve Vidler/Leo de Wys, Inc.; back cover: ©Mike
Lichter/International Stock Photo; title page and pages 28, 36, 40: ©Alain Evrard/Photo
Researchers, Inc.; pages 6, 32, 50, 53: ©Fridmar Damm/Leo de Wys, Inc.; pages 9, 46: Chad
Ehlers/International Stock Photo; page 11: ©Michele & Tom Grimm/International Stock
Photo; page 13: North Wind Picture Archives; page 16: ©Paul Chesley/Tony Stone
Worldwide; page 21: ©Alain Le Garsmeur/Tony Stone Worldwide; page 22: ©John
Elk/Tony Stone Images, Inc.; page 24: ©Stock, Boston/Nathan Benn/PNI; page 25: ©Tony
Stone Worldwide; page 31: ©Herb Schmitz/Tony Stone Images; page 35: ©Stock,
Boston/D. H. Hessell/PNI; page 38: ©Rick Browne/Photo Researchers, Inc.; page 43:
©Robert E. Daemmrich/Tony Stone Worldwide; page 44: ©H. Edward Kim/National
Geographic Society; page 45: ©Stock, Boston/Bob Daemmrich/PNI; page 48: ©David
Burnett/Leo de Wys, Inc.; page 54: ©Orion/International Stock Photo; page 55: ©Robin
Laurance/Photo Researchers, Inc.

Contents

Map of Korea..Frontispiece

1 GEOGRAPHY AND HISTORY
Mountains High and Beautiful 7

2 THE PEOPLE
Living and Working Together 17

3 FAMILY LIFE, FESTIVALS, AND FOOD
The Respectful Culture 29

4 SCHOOL LIFE AND RECREATION
Loving to Learn . . . and Play 41

5 THE ARTS
A Creative People..47

Country Facts..56

Glossary..60

For Further Reading..62

Index..63

Korea is a beautiful land. Here, pavilions in the South Korean city of Kwangju are reflected in a pond at sunset.

1
GEOGRAPHY AND HISTORY

Mountains High and Beautiful

Tangun, Son of Bear-Woman

About 4,000 years ago, a bear and a tiger decided that they were tired of being animals. They wanted to be humans. They prayed and prayed to the Divine Creator, Hwanin (hwan-een).* Eventually, Hwanung (hwan-oong), the Divine Creator's son, heard their prayers and came down to earth from heaven, landing next to a sandalwood tree on Mount Paektusan. He became king of all the people.

To help the bear and the tiger get their wish, Hwanung gave them each a bitter-tasting piece of magic wormwood to eat. He also gave them twenty helpings of smelly garlic. If they would eat these plants, he said, and stay out of the sunlight for one hundred days, they would turn into human beings.

The bear and the tiger were so excited about becoming humans that they gladly ate the bitter food. Then they went to live in a dark cave. But the tiger didn't like staying inside the cave for such a long

* Although we are used to stressing one syllable in a word more than the others, the Korean language generally does not do so.

7

time. He gave up and went outside to run around in the sunshine. He did not turn into a human. The bear, however, had more patience, and after a long time, she turned into a woman.

The first wish that the bear-woman had when she came out of the cave was to have a baby. But she had no husband because the tiger had not turned into a man. She climbed up to the top of Mount Paektusan and found the sandalwood tree with its delicious, perfumelike scent. There she prayed and prayed. Her wish was granted by the God-King Hwanung, who married her himself. She named their baby boy Tangun (tan-goon). Tangun would be the first human being to become king of the people of Korea.

Land of Many Mountains

Today, people do not believe that Korea (ko-ree-uh) was first ruled by the son of a bear-woman. But some Koreans still remember the legend of Tangun and celebrate the day he was said to have been crowned, some 4,000 years ago.

Korea is an ancient land. It lies on the eastern coast of the continent of Asia. To the south, salty ocean waves crash against thousands of rocky islands. The sea spray rises high into the air. In the north, sparkling snowflakes settle gently on the pine needles of the Mountain of Eternal Snow. In the valleys, cherry trees explode with bright pink blossoms. In the lakes, lotus flowers float quietly on the water. And there are caves so large and deep that they seem like upside-down mountains.

The name *Korea* comes from the word *Koryo*, which means "high and clear." Koreans also like to call their country *Choson* (cho-sun)—the "land of the morning calm." Korea is a peninsula, a land surrounded on three sides by water. The shallow Yellow Sea is on the west side, the deep Sea of Japan is on the

Mist covers the mountains in Soraksan National Park, located in north-eastern South Korea.

east side, and the windy Korea Strait lies to the south. Korea is connected at its northern end to China and Russia. The next-nearest country to Korea is Japan.

Two large mountain ranges stretch up and down the peninsula. Smaller mountain ranges run east and west. Put together, these mountains take up most of the land, about 70 percent, leaving the rest for farmlands, cities, and towns. Korean children love to go hiking in the mountains with their parents or friends. They especially like to hike in the fall, when the leaves turn yellow, red, and brown.

The tallest mountain on the Korean peninsula is Paektusan (peck-too-san), or "Mountain of Eternal Snow." Located in the north, on the border with China, it is 9,003 feet (2,744 meters) high. Paektusan is actually a volcano, but smoke, gas, and lava no longer come out of it. Instead, a beautiful lake, called the Lake of Heaven, sparkles in the volcano's crater.

In the southern part of Korea, some of the mountains are partly underwater. The tops poke out of the sea to make rocky islands. There are more than 3,500 such islands.

Flowing Ribbons of Water

Korea has many rivers, some large and some small. The Yalu (yah-loo) River, which flows into the Yellow Sea, is one of the major rivers. It is very long and wide. Along with the Tumen (too-mehn) River, which flows into the Sea of Japan, the Yalu separates Korea from China and Russia. In the northern part of Korea, the Taedong (teh-dong) River is important to farmers, who use the water to irrigate their rice fields.

Korea's rivers are also useful for generating electricity. Koreans have built dams on some rivers. They let the water out of the dams little by little. The power of the flowing water is changed into electricity by large machines called turbines. The electricity is sent through wires to homes, stores, schools, and offices so that people's lights, fans, radios, televisions, and other appliances will work.

Because most of Korea's rivers flow westward, toward the Yellow Sea, the people on the eastern side of the country have not had enough electricity. A few years ago, government engineers were actually able to reverse the flow of several rivers. They cut tunnels through the mountains and sent the water the opposite way, toward the Sea of Japan.

Now Koreans on the east side of the country have more water and enough electricity.

Cold Winters, Wet Summers

Korean children must be ready for very different kinds of weather. Korea is not far from Siberia, a part of Russia that is one of the coldest places on earth. Beginning in November, winds from Siberia bring snow to Korea's mountains and cold, dry air to its valleys. Warm coats, hats, and gloves are necessary for the cold winters. Then, in July, warm, wet air from the Pacific Ocean blows across the land. Sometimes it rains almost every day for a month. During this time, the rivers overflow their banks, and some cities are struck with floods. This rainy period is called the monsoon season. Monsoon rains are important for farmers, especially for those who grow rice. Rice needs a lot of water. It is grown in paddies, fields that are soaked with water. Farmers have been growing rice in Korea for thousands of years.

Paddies must be flooded with water for rice to grow.

Korea Long Ago

The Korean people have a saying that describes their history: "When the big whales fight, the small shrimps suffer." In ancient times, Korean people controlled a lot of land in the area that is now China and Mongolia. But Korea has usually been a "small shrimp" in Asia, while China, Mongolia, Russia, and Japan have been the "big whales."

More than 2,000 years ago, for example, Chinese soldiers invaded parts of northern Korea. The Korean tribes living in the area were not able to keep the Chinese out of their country. The Chinese ruled over part of Korea for almost 400 years. During this time, many ideas entered Korea from China. Koreans began to copy the Chinese style of painting and writing. They built Chinese-style homes and made Chinese-style bowls, weapons, and chariots. The Koreans learned many valuable things from the Chinese, but they did not have freedom.

Kingdoms of Old

When China's power began to weaken, Koreans formed three kingdoms of their own. One, in the north, was called Koguryo (ko-gu-rio). The other two were in the south. They were called Silla (shil-lah) and Paekche (peck-cheh). The people in these three kingdoms fought against one another for many years. Finally, Silla, with the help of the Chinese, unified the country under its control in A.D. 668.

Silla controlled Korea for more than 250 years. Then, a thousand years ago, a powerful ruling family arose in the land. They became known as the Koryo (ko-rio) dynasty. (A dynasty is a family that stays in power for a very long time.) It is from the Koryo dynasty that we have the name *Korea* today.

After nearly 300 years of independence, in about the year 1231, Korea was invaded again—this time by the horse-riding Mongols from the north. The Mongols then ruled the land. Eventually, the Koreans drove out the Mongols.

12

When General Yi Song-gye took power in 1392, he made Seoul his new capital city.

New Rulers

In 1392, General Yi Song-gye (ee sawng-gay) and his troops took control of the Korean government, founding the Yi (ee) dynasty. Korea was renamed *Choson*—an ancient name for Korea—and the Choson era began. But in the late 1500s, the Japanese attacked, capturing many cities, including Seoul (sohl). This was the city that housed the royal palace. Originally, the Japanese had wanted to attack China and had asked the Koreans to help them. But when the Koreans refused to help, the Japanese attacked them instead.

To defend the Korean Navy against the Japanese, an admiral named Yi Sun-sin (ee sun-shin) decided to put a coat of heavy iron on the sides of his ships. This stopped the Japanese cannonballs from sinking the ships. The iron ships were so effective that Admiral Yi was able to sink more than 500 Japanese ships, while most of his ships remained safe.

The Korean people had never seen ships with iron sides before. Before, all ships had been made of wood. The iron coating on the ships reminded the people of the hard, protective shell of turtles. They called them *gobugson* (ga-book-sun), turtle ships. Since then, Admiral Yi has been considered a hero by the Korean people.

13

The turtle ships helped to hold off the Japanese, but they were not defeated until the Koreans received help from China. From then on, although China did not actually control Korea, it had a lot of power over Korean leaders. Korean people gradually adopted more Chinese customs.

Three hundred years later, in 1895, Japan beat China in another war. China then agreed to stop trying to control Korea.

Then Russia wanted to control Korea. But in 1905, Russia lost a war to Japan and did not have the power to control Korea. So, in 1910, Japan officially took control of Korea. For the next thirty-six years, Japan ruled the country. The Korean people were forced to change their names to Japanese names. Korean children had to speak Japanese in school and were made to bow to pictures of the Japanese emperor. Sunjong (soon-jong), the Korean emperor, had to give up his throne. He died in 1926, and there have been no Korean emperors since then.

Out of One, Two

When Japan lost World War II to the United States and the other Allies in 1945, it had to give up its control of Korea. Koreans hoped that they would have a truly free country at last. Russia still wanted to control the northern section, however. Russia helped some Koreans in the north create a country called the Democratic People's Republic of Korea, or North Korea.

The people in the south created a different country, called the Republic of Korea, or South Korea. When soldiers from the north tried to take over the new country, the United Nations stopped them by sending soldiers, including thousands of Americans. This struggle was called the Korean War. It lasted from 1950 to 1953, and many people lost their lives.

At the end of the war, Korea was still divided into two countries. Russia gave money and food to the North Koreans, while the United States and fifteen other countries of the United Nations gave money and food to the South Koreans. Today, a long double wall of barbed wire, with soldiers on each side, keeps the North Koreans and South Koreans apart. Until recently, no one from either side was allowed to visit the other. Even now, only a few people are allowed to visit their families on opposite sides of the wire wall.

KOREAN GOVERNMENTS

Korea is divided into two countries, North Korea and South Korea. Their governments are very different. The North Korean government appears to be run by the Korean people. There is a Supreme People's Assembly, which passes laws, and a president, who is elected to four-year terms. All citizens aged seventeen and older can vote.

Political power, however, is not really held by the voters. Instead, the Communist Korean Workers' party holds the power, and the head of the Communist party is the president of the country. Though the full name of the country is the Democratic People's Republic of Korea, it is not actually a democracy, in which people can say what they want and change the government if they choose. North Koreans are not allowed to say things against the government. If they do, they are punished. Some are put in jail, and some are executed. This kind of government is a dictatorship.

In South Korea, the people can choose their president in free elections. Everyone can vote at age twenty. The president may serve for only five years, and then someone else must be elected. South Korea has several political parties, each with different ideas about how the country should be governed. The Constitution, a formal set of rules for running the country, gives a lot of power to the president. Elected members of the National Assembly also have much power to make laws. South Korea is a representative democracy.

Today, many South Koreans work in cities. Many run businesses, such as this textile shop in Seoul, which sells silks.

2
THE PEOPLE

Living and Working Together

Long before the first kingdom of Korea was started, small tribes of Asian people lived all over the Korean peninsula and in what is now northeast China. Many lived in caves or simple shelters. They hunted for animals using spears tipped with sharp stones. Mostly, they fished, with nets and spears.

Who were these people, and where did they come from? Nobody knows for sure. People did not read or write 5,000 years ago, so the early Koreans did not record their history. However, some scientists today believe that the early Koreans came to the peninsula from a region north of China, from the country now known as Mongolia.

The People Who Kept to Themselves
Korean children have straight black hair. They used to think that everyone in the world looked just like they did because they rarely saw a person with blond, brown, or curly black hair.

For a long time, the Korean government refused to let other people into the country. It did not even want to buy things from foreigners. By experience, the government had learned that other countries wanted to control Korea, so the leaders thought that it was safer to stay away from people from other countries. Korea became an isolated country.

Even today, most of the 69 million people who live on the Korean peninsula are native Koreans. They are mostly descendants of the first people to settle in the peninsula. This sameness is unusual in the modern world. Most citizens of Australia, Canada, and the United States, for example, can trace their heritage to many other parts of the world. Their ancestors were born in Europe, Africa, Latin America, the South Pacific, and Asia. But except for some people from China and other parts of Asia, and some American soldiers, most of the people living in Korea are descendants of the early inhabitants.

Because of television, movies, and computer networks, Koreans are learning about people of other lands. Some Koreans have moved to other countries. Four million Koreans now live outside of Korea.

The Language Invented by a King

Koreans today are very proud of their written language. But for hundreds of years, they had no alphabet. In 1446, a Korean king named Sejong decided that it was time to invent an alphabet. Today, the system that he had court scholars invent is called *han'gul* (hawn-gool) in South Korea and *choson muntcha* (cho-soon mun-cha) in North Korea. The alphabet has ten vowels and fourteen consonants. The characters look something like Chinese characters, but, instead of words, they stand for sounds.

Koreans form sentences by putting the subject first and the verb last. For example, instead of saying, "I am going to school," Koreans say, "I to school am going." Here are a few Korean words to try on your friends:

Hello (on meeting)	*Annyong* (an-young)
Hello? (on phone)	*Yobaseayo* (yo-boh-seh-yo)
Thank you	*Kamsahamnida* (kam-sa-ham-nee-dah)
Excuse me	*Shillyehamnida* (shil-leh-ham-nee-dah)
Teacher	*Songsang* (sun-sang)
Father	*Aboji* (ah-boh-jee)
Mother	*Omani* (oh-moh-nee)
Yes	*ye* (yeh) or *ne* (neh)
No	*Ano* (an-yo)
Good-bye	*Annyonghikasaeyo* (an-young-hee-keh-seh-yo)

In South Korea, many Korean words, such as family names, are still written in Chinese. In fact, more than half of the words in Korean come from Chinese.

The Korean people, however, prefer their own writing system. They have been using the *han'gul* alphabet for more than 500 years, and almost 96 percent of the South Korean people and 99 percent of the North Koreans can read and write it. Koreans are so proud of their writing system that they celebrate National Language Day in October.

Study Hard or Stay Where You Are

For a long time, Koreans believed that some people were naturally better than others. Government leaders were believed to be better than soldiers. Farmers were thought to be better than shopkeepers. And, in turn, shopkeepers were thought to be better than servants and slaves.

When groups of people think that they are different from, or better than, other types of people, we say that they believe in a class system. In countries with class systems, there are usually big differences in how much power and money various groups of people have.

In ancient Korea, usually only rich people could afford to send their children to school. Rich people and their families were called *yangban* (yang-bahn). The farmers worked for them and paid rent to them. The rich people had many privileges. They did not have to pay taxes to the government, for example, and they did not have to become soldiers.

Under the class system, people stay within their group. It's very difficult to move up to a higher class. The children of *yangban* families, for example, would not marry farmers, and the children of farm families would not marry shopkeepers.

Following Confucius

Korean people lived in this strict class system mainly because of the teachings of a famous Chinese philosopher named Confucius. Confucius lived about 2,500 years ago. For hundreds of years, Korean people followed his teachings. He taught that each person was different but that, if the members of each class behaved according to their role in society—that is, if the leaders would be good leaders and the farmers would be good farmers—then life would be better for everyone.

Confucius, however, also taught that people from any group could enter the highest level of society if they passed difficult written tests. Generally, only the best-educated Koreans—usually the rich—could pass them. Sometimes, though, children of poorer families were able to pass them. Because of this possibility, Korean parents made their children study hard.

These young girls, in matching uniforms, line up in pairs, ready to enter school and study hard.

Today, most Koreans no longer believe in the old Confucian class system. They believe that all people are created equal. But the tradition of getting ahead by studying hard remains. Because of this tradition, Korean children sometimes get the highest grades on international examinations in mathematics and science. As far as Korean parents are concerned, the best way that children can show respect for them is to study hard.

Spirits and Shamans

In addition to following the teachings of Confucius, ancient Koreans believed that everything—even rocks, trees, and mountains—had spirits in them. This belief, called animism, was held by many peoples around the world. To make the spirits happy or to stop them from doing harm, people would ask the help of a shaman, or priest. In Korea, shamans were

21

Shamanists believe that all things in nature have spirits. These posts honor such spirits.

usually women. They would dance, sing, and chant prayers to the spirits.

Some Koreans today think that animism, also called shamanism, is just superstition. But there are still people who practice shamanism every day.

In South Korea, more than half of the people follow religions such as Buddhism and Christianity. In North Korea, where the government discourages people from practicing any religion, there are still some individuals who believe in Buddhism. Many also follow the teachings of Confucius.

Korean Christians

In 1794, the first Christian missionaries went to Korea to try to convert people to their religious beliefs. Many Koreans joined Christian churches. The government was afraid of Christianity because it was a foreign religion.

Today, Christianity is very strong in South Korea. In fact, there are more Christians living in South Korea than in any other Asian country except the Philippines. Korean Christians have built churches, hospitals, and schools. They have also been important in the human rights movement.

Some Koreans are members of churches that combine the teachings of Christianity with the teachings of both Buddhism and Confucianism. One example of this is a religion called Ch'ondogyo (chun-do-gyo), which means "Religion of the Heavenly Way."

Making Money: Two Different Korean Ways

In North Korea, the government decides what kinds of companies there should be and how many products each company should make. Private enterprise is not allowed. Also, the North Korean government has forbidden its people from trading much with other nations. Instead, the people have been told to make their own things. This plan is called *juche* (joo-cheh), or self-reliance.

In South Korea, companies are privately owned. The government does not control them. Also, companies are free to sell their products to other countries. South Koreans may also buy things from other countries.

Which system has worked better? Most people think that South Korea has been more successful. Stores in South Korea are filled with things to buy, and South Koreans earn more money than North Koreans do. People live longer in South Korea than in North Korea because of better nutrition and health care. Newborn babies are healthier. More families have telephones and newspapers. It is easier to go places because there are more roads and airports.

City Life and Farm Life

You probably have some South Korean products in your house or garage. Maybe you have a Samsung television set. Perhaps your parents drive a Hyundai automobile. Out of every one hundred South Korean workers, seventy-nine work in cities where such products are made. Only twenty-one out of every one hundred people work on farms in South Korea, but the South Koreans still have more food to eat than the North Koreans. Thirty-nine out of every one hundred North Koreans live and work on farms, but they often do not have enough to eat.

Some farmers, especially in North Korea, are very poor. They live in villages where the roads are just dusty paths and the houses are roofed with straw. Other farmers, especially those in South Korea, live well. They plant their rice with automatic planting machines. They can afford to buy fertilizer

Farmwork, especially in North Korea, is very hard, with much of it still done by people rather than machines.

Seoul, lit up at dusk, sparkles against the mountains.

to help their crops grow. They harvest their grain with large, modern equipment.

Korean farmers' main crops are rice and barley. They also raise corn, potatoes, and soybeans. They grow fruit in their orchards, especially juicy apples and sweet peaches. Many Koreans own boats and fish for a living. The ocean on the west side of the Korean peninsula has many good places to fish.

Seoul, the capital of South Korea, is a modern city with tall glass-and-steel skyscrapers, large apartment buildings, and many stores. Pyongyang, the capital of North Korea, is also a beautiful, clean city, but it is not as modern or as large as Seoul.

South Koreans work very hard making ships, cars, and clothing. Many South Korean men are welders, designers, and construction workers. The women often work making

This shopkeeper displays many kinds of dried fish—including a huge dried squid.

clothing or shoes, as assemblers of electronic products such as televisions, or as secretaries and shop clerks. Both North and South Koreans work six days a week, and some take no week-end break. But the South Korean worker makes more than six times as much money as the North Korean worker does because of the differences in their countries' economies.

Many people think it would be better for the North Koreans if their country traded more things with foreign nations. The only country that North Korea trades very much with is its neighbor China. People also think it would be better if North Korea spent less money on its army. For every one dollar that North Koreans make, their government spends from twelve to twenty-five cents for its military. In comparison, the South Korean government spends only three cents per dollar on its military. As a result, there is more money left in South Korea to build schools, better roads, and nice public buildings such as museums and theaters.

Fashions, Old and New

Almost all Korean children and their parents wear the same kinds of clothes that people in, say, Canada and the United States wear: blue jeans, T-shirts, sneakers, suits and ties for men, and dresses and high heels for women.

On holidays and special occasions such as weddings, however, Korean people usually wear traditional clothing called *hanbok* (han-bok). The women and girls wear long silk dresses called *chima* (chee-ma). These dresses are tied high above the waist and may be of any color: bright yellow or red, pure white, deep purple, lush pink, or sky blue. They wear many layers of undergarments to make the *chima* appear big and full. They also wear blouses that are tied in front and have long sleeves. In their braided hair, the women wear bright ribbons. On their feet, they wear flat, comfortable shoes. Some women, however, choose to wear Western-style bridal gowns when they marry.

These young women are wearing brightly colored traditional dresses.

Men, even for special occasions, usually dress in suits and ties. But sometimes they wear a traditional outfit: long, baggy pants underneath a long coat that ties in front.

Traditional dance and costumes are part of the Royal Confucian Ceremony in Seoul.

3
FAMILY LIFE, FESTIVALS, AND FOOD

The Respectful Culture

Mrs. Pak is about to have her first baby. For nine months, she has followed the Korean traditions for pregnant women. She has not eaten squid, eggs, duck, or the skin of chickens. She has eaten seaweed soup. She has prayed to the grandmother spirit responsible for childbirth. She has reported her dreams to relatives, who have tried to guess whether the baby will be a boy or a girl. Dreams about horses or tigers are believed to mean a boy, while dreams about flowers mean a girl.

For good luck, Mrs. Pak is dressed in the clothing of a neighbor who had a very easy time delivering a baby. As a result, maybe Mrs. Pak will have an easy time, too. Some Korean women go to hospitals to have their babies, but Mrs. Pak will give birth at home. Mrs. Pak's husband has given some of his clothes to use as covers on the bed, another way to ensure good luck.

At last, the moment has come: Mrs. Pak gives birth to a baby boy. The parents name him Cheahan (chay-han). All the people who are there to help—the grandmothers, aunts, nieces, and of course, the father—are very happy about the new family member. The father hangs a string of red peppers on the gate of the house. This lets people know that a baby boy has been born. (For a girl, he would hang a rope made from straw and charcoal.) These things also are supposed to keep disease and evil spirits away from the new baby. (Many people today no longer follow these practices.)

For one week after the birth, Mrs. Pak eats seaweed soup and rice seven times a day to help her regain her strength. After one hundred days, the family holds a celebration, called a *paik-il* (peck-ill) party, with friends and relatives. There, they eat rice cakes, called *ddok* (dock), and sweet bean cakes. At Cheahan's first year's birthday party, he is placed before a table filled with food, money, books, sewing thread, and a rainbow-layered cake, called *moo jee gae ddok* (moo gee gay dock). All the family members watch to see which object he picks up first. If he picks up money, it means that he will be rich when he grows up. If he picks up a book, he will be a good student in school. If he picks up the thread, he will live to be very old.

The Center of the Culture

To Koreans, the family is the most important thing in the world. Today, fathers work in companies and mothers either stay at home with their two or three children or work outside the home. But traditional Korean families were different. In the old days, many homes had twelve or more people living together, including aunts, uncles, grandparents, cousins, and servants. They all worked together on their farm. To live together peaceably, the members of these extended families obeyed rules taught by Confucius. The rules made it clear who had authority in the home. Children had to obey their parents. Wives were supposed to obey their husbands. Servants were expected to obey their masters. And all younger people were required to respect all older people.

Respect for the elderly is an important part of Korean life.

The father was the head of the house. When he died, the oldest son, not the mother, became the head of the house. When the children grew up and married, the younger brothers and sisters moved away, but the oldest son and his wife stayed in the family home and raised their own children there. The oldest son was also in charge of performing prayers for the father and other ancestors who had died. Many Korean families today still follow these traditions, but some do not.

Most modern Korean families are not as large as families were in the old days. Some Koreans live in small apartments that are big enough only for the parents and perhaps two children. The old-style homes had tile roofs and straw mats on the floor. In contrast, modern apartments look like apartment buildings in Canada and the United States. Inside, there may be a sofa, a television, a refrigerator, and other modern furnishings. One custom that has not changed, however, is that people take their shoes off before they enter the house.

Recent laws in both North Korea and South Korea have created more equality between women and men. As a result, some women have been elected to important positions in government. Other women work as lawyers, judges, and newspaper reporters. In North Korea, the government pays for day-care centers for the children of working mothers.

Still, at home, the traditions of the past continue. After work, most mothers, even those who have jobs outside the home, take care of the children and the house. Fathers usually work long hours, including Saturdays, at their jobs.

Keeping the Family History

Along with his other duties, the oldest son was responsible for recording the family history. Even today, a record has to be made of every child born into the family, every marriage, and every death. In the old days, these records were especially important to rich families who wanted to prove that their clan

In this wedding party, the bride and groom wear traditional clothes and are surrounded by objects meant to bring love, health, and long life.

was related to the king. *Clan,* or *sseajok* (sea-joke), is the term given to all the people who are members of an extended family, including cousins, uncles, aunts, and in-laws. In the past, certain clans were given special privileges by the government. People paid a lot of attention to their family genealogy, or history records. Today, some clans in Korea can trace their family histories back nearly 2,000 years.

The New Year's Day That Lasts Two Weeks

One of the most important holidays for Koreans is the celebration of the new year. On New Year's Day, January 1, children and parents dress in new clothes. They visit the houses of grandparents, older relatives, or other people they respect and wish them good luck in the new year. They bow to the oldest person first, then to the next oldest, and so on. The grandparents often give the children some *won* (wan), or Korean money. Then the family enjoys a large dinner, including rice-dough soup. Drinking the soup is a symbol that everyone is becoming one year older.

Families also play many games during the celebration. They fly kites and play Korean chess. Some families continue these activities for as long as two weeks! Everyone takes off work and school for at least a few days. On the night of the fifteenth day of the New Year, children and their parents hike up a mountain and bow to the moon. This is their way of asking for their new year's wishes to come true.

The Harvest Moon Festival

There is another time during the year when children and their parents hike up mountains at night. This is in September or October during the full moon. Farmers in particular like the

Harvest Moon Festival, or *Chusok* (chu-sohk)—the Korean Thanksgiving, because it marks the end of their season. They get to rest from their hard work and enjoy the harvest. Women wearing beautiful traditional dresses sometimes perform a circle dance under the full moon.

The most important part of this festival is visiting the graves of relatives who have died. Family members from all over return home to visit the graves of grandparents and other relatives. Many families have private cemeteries in which only their relatives are buried. Each person bows respectfully before the graves, and then everyone shares a nighttime meal.

Honoring Kings and Queens

People who are related to some of the former kings and queens of the Yi dynasty (the last royal family to rule Korea) hold a special celebration the first Sunday of each May. They gather at the Chyongmyo (choung-mo) T'aeje Temple in Seoul. The six-hour formal ceremony includes court music and dance. They wear long black, red, and white robes and black and gold hats, which make them look like Confucian monks. They say prayers while standing at attention, and then they bow to the family records that are kept in the temple. The records contain a list of the names and activities of the twenty-seven Yi kings and queens of Korea. Many people come to watch this famous ceremony.

Liberation and Other Ceremonies

Since the northern and southern parts of the Korean peninsula are ruled by different governments, national holidays vary. Both Christmas and Buddha's birthday are celebrated in the

Many South Koreans are Buddhists. Their temples are decorated with statues of Buddha, who lived about 2,500 years ago.

south, for example, but not in the north. However, there is at least one holiday that all Koreans observe: Liberation Day. This is held on August 15 to celebrate the day in 1945 that the Japanese stopped controlling Korea. For thirty-six years, the Japanese had ruled Korea. During that time, they tried to keep people from speaking the Korean language, and they took over all the top positions in the government.

Today, South Koreans cooperate with the Japanese on many things. They buy many products from Japan. Even North Korea sometimes buys rice and other food from Japan. But all Koreans, from north and south, still celebrate the day that the Japanese left their country. They hold big parades, wave their national flags, and take a day off from work.

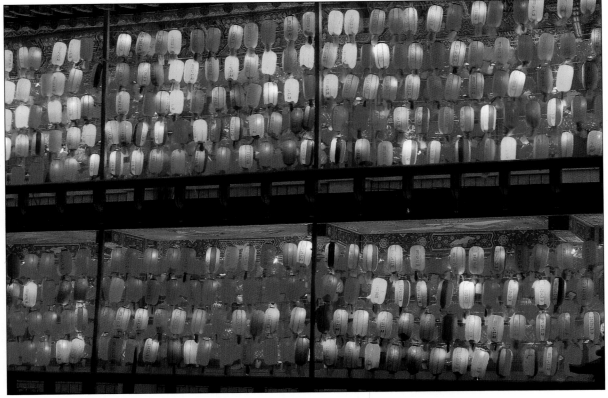

The Toson Temple in Seoul is decorated for Buddha's birthday.

Another important holiday is Children's Day, which is May 5. On this day, parents and children, dressed in traditional Korean clothing, crowd public parks to play games and have picnics. This used to be called Boy's Day, but now the celebration is for both boys and girls.

Korean Foods: Tasty and Hot

Korean foods are hot and spicy. Red peppers and onions are mixed with all kinds of grains, vegetables, meat, or fish. Most meals also include some kind of soup, such as bean-sprout soup, and every meal includes steamed rice. In fact, almost all Koreans eat steamed rice every day, three times a day.

KIMCHI: A FAVORITE SIDE DISH

5 cups cabbage, cut into
  bite-size pieces
6 tablespoons salt
2 tablespoons sugar
1 teaspoon to 2 tablespoons
  crushed red pepper flakes

1/4 teaspoon finely chopped
  ginger root
1 clove garlic, peeled and
  finely chopped
2 green onions, finely chopped

1. In a large colander, mix the cabbage together with 5 tablespoons of salt. Let it sit for about three hours.
2. Rinse cabbage two or three times. Then squeeze out the excess liquid with your hands.
3. Place the drained cabbage in a large glass bowl. Then add the remaining ingredients and mix together.
4. Cover the cabbage mixture tightly with plastic wrap and let it sit at room temperature for two days.
5. Chill before serving.

This recipe makes about 5 cups of kimchi.

Probably the most famous Korean dish to go with rice is kimchi (kim-chee). Kimchi is usually made from pickled Chinese cabbage. The white cabbage is sprinkled with salt and left to sit for several days. Garlic, cucumbers, green onions, oysters, salted fish, ginger, red peppers, and turnips are then added.

Another delicious Korean dish is called *bulgogi* (bull-go-key). A major ingredient of *bulgogi* is beef. The meat is cut into thin strips and soaked in a mixture of black pepper, onions, garlic, and sesame oil. Then it is broiled on a special metal grill right on the table, dipped in soy sauce, and eaten with chopsticks. Of course, it, too, is served with steamed rice.

When you first sit down to dinner in a Korean home, you may think that there are very few rules to obey. For instance, it is acceptable to put your elbows on the table and to make slurping noises while you eat. You do not have to sit up straight in your chair because you eat while sitting on the floor. And you may not actually be sitting at a table but in front of an individual wooden tray. You do not have to ask "please" to receive the soy sauce; you just take it. And you do not have to eat food in any particular order, such as salad first, main course second, and so on. Instead, all the food is placed on the table or on individual trays at once for everyone to eat in any order they wish.

The many dishes on this table make up dinner for two, including bulgogi *(on grill) and* kimchi *(to left of the fish on the bottom right).*

But, as you might expect, there are some very important table rules to follow. The oldest person must be allowed to start eating before younger people do and must be allowed to finish eating before younger people get up from the table. Traditionally, men were served first. Women waited on them and ate only when the men were done. Today, families eat together. It is not polite for anyone to talk very much during the meal, and people should not poke chopsticks straight up into their rice bowls or pour their own drinks. People should pour drinks for others but not for themselves.

Fast-food restaurants line this Seoul street.

Hamburgers, Anyone?

Korean people love their own food, but they also like foods of
other countries. Restaurants serve Chinese food, Russian food,
Japanese food, and North American food. Especially in Seoul,
people can go to fast-food restaurants and buy hamburgers,
French fries, pizzas, and soft drinks. These fast-food restaurants are especially popular among young Koreans.

Korean teens study hard all week long, but on Sundays they enjoy leisure activities such as roller-skating.

4
SCHOOL LIFE AND RECREATION

Loving to Learn
. . . and Play

Schools in Korea are filled with children, teachers, desks, books, and all the other usual things. But they are also filled with respect. Hundreds of years ago, students called their teachers *sabu*, which means "teaching father." In other words, teachers were considered almost as important as parents. Today teachers are still highly respected, though they are not very well paid.

Parents teach their children to be polite when talking to their teachers. When handing in papers, students must get up from their seats and go to the teacher's desk. Students do not expect the teacher to come to them. They must hold their paper with two hands and bow to the teacher while turning it in.

Chewing gum in school, putting feet up on the desk, forgetting to bring a pencil, and being absent are simply not acceptable, because they show disrespect to the teacher. Koreans have a saying about respect for teachers. They say that "teachers are so important that a person should not even step on their shadows."

A Day at School

Korean students begin the school day by having an assembly outside on the playground. They stand at attention while the principal makes announcements. Then the students bow, thank the principal, and go off to class.

Class is much like it is in North America. Students sit at desks facing the blackboard. They study arithmetic, science, the Korean language, history, art, and music. They work on projects in small groups. The average elementary school class has about sixty students—both boys and girls. Students often eat lunch at their desks because there is no cafeteria.

After school, the children divide into groups and clean the school building. They empty the wastebaskets, sweep the floors and hallways, and pick up trash on the school grounds. At home, they have lots of homework to do. In fact, homework is so important that many parents do not ask their children to do any chores at home so that they will have plenty of time to study.

A Devotion to Learning

In North Korea, students may stop going to school after high school. In South Korea, after attending elementary school and several years of junior high school, children may stop going to school. The law does not require students to attend high school at all, but almost all South Korean students go to high school. Parents consider school so important that they will sell their homes and move to another part of town with better schools if they think their neighborhood schools are not good enough.

The average high school class in South Korea has sixty students. The students stay in one room, and the teachers

In a South Korean high school, these students learn computer skills.

move from room to room. High schools are usually all boys or all girls, not mixed. In the past, all high school students had to wear uniforms. Some schools still require this, but most students now wear jeans, sneakers, and shirts or blouses.

During the last year of high school, students who want to go to college must take a very difficult examination. This test is so hard that students spend almost all their spare time studying for it. They do not date, baby-sit, or have part-time jobs. If they pass the exam, they may go to college. If they do not pass, they will go to work at a company or take special classes at night school to learn a skill.

Time Out for Games

Korean children work hard at school. But on holidays, they take time off and enjoy playing games with their families and friends. Girls love to seesaw and to swing. Boys love to wrestle. Both boys and girls enjoy gymnastics and folk dancing.

Chajonnori (cha-john-no-ree) is a game that many young men like to play. The players divide into two groups. One person from each side climbs up tall, V-shaped wooden platforms while the crowd rams the platforms together. The idea is to knock off the opposite player. The player who can hold

South Korean teenage gymnasts participate in a national athletics competition.

on longer wins. To North Americans, the game looks much like king-of-the-hill.

Another popular activity is kite flying. People like to fly kites around New Year's time. First, they make the kites out of thin paper and strips of bamboo. They then write the names of evil spirits and diseases on them. When they send the kites into the sky, all the unpleasant things are carried away. Two people sometimes send their kites up at the same time. They attach the strings on the ground. When the kites are high in the sky, they let them crash into each other. Sometimes, the kites stay tangled together for hours. The person whose kite string breaks first is the loser.

While the children are seesawing, swinging (usually done standing up, not sitting down), and flying kites, the adult men play *changgi* (chang-gee), or Korean chess. Each player has sixteen pieces, including horses, elephants, chariots, soldiers, and a general. The goal is to trap the general of the opposite side so that the general cannot move.

Taekwondo **and Other Sports**

Among the team sports brought into Korea from other countries, baseball is the most popular, followed by soccer. There are professional teams for both sports. Koreans get very excited watching games on television, just as North Americans do during the Super Bowl or World Series. Koreans also like to play volleyball, basketball, and Ping-Pong.

Koreans are especially proud of one of their own sports: *taekwondo* (teh-kwan-doe). Like karate and judo (*yudo* [you-doe] in Korean), *taekwondo* is very popular among boys and young men. It started in Korea well over a thousand years ago as a way for people to defend themselves from personal attack.

Ssirum (she-room) is the Korean form of Japanese sumo wrestling. In *ssirum* wrestling, two men stand inside a small circle and, while holding on to each other, try to knock each other down. The winner of a series of these contests is called the "strongest man under heaven." Koreans across the nation enjoy watching these matches on television.

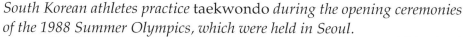

South Korean athletes practice taekwondo *during the opening ceremonies of the 1988 Summer Olympics, which were held in Seoul.*

Celadon pottery is one of the most well-known Korean art forms.

5

THE ARTS

A Creative People

Korean artists are skilled at making beautiful objects from wood. Sometimes they make boxes with a lacquer, or high polish, finish. To make this lacquerware, the artists first attach cloth to a wooden box. They use layers of rice glue, charcoal powder, and varnish to attach the cloth. Then they sand and polish the black surface until it is very smooth. Finally, they carve designs in the surface and put pieces of shiny mother-of-pearl in the carved-out spaces.

Probably the most famous art object that Koreans make is celadon pottery. It comes in many forms, including bowls, plates, flower vases, and cups. After shaping the wet clay, the artists, called potters, put their work in a kiln, a special pottery oven. As it bakes, the clay becomes very hard. After it cools, the potters paint a colorful, shiny glaze on the surface. Sometimes they add tiny pictures of birds, mountains, or trees. Then they put the object back into the oven. When it comes out, it is like beautiful glass. It often has tiny broken lines or cracks under the surface. Some people mistakenly

Masked dancers act out a story.

think the bowl or cup is broken, but actually, the tiny lines are there on purpose, to add to the beauty. Celadon pottery can come in many colors, but the most famous is a light blue-green.

Masked Dances and Ancient Tales

Masked dance performances probably started hundreds of years ago. They began as an expression of spiritual belief but then became a way for poor people to make fun of rich people without getting into trouble. Farmers made masks with ugly faces on them and then pretended that they were rich noblemen who were not very smart or Buddhist monks who were not very religious. They would dance and act out a funny story. Traditionally, the masks were burned after the performance because they were thought to be contaminated by evil spirits. This is still one of the most popular types of drama in Korea today.

Similar to masked-dance drama is an art form called *pansori* (pan-so-ree). *Pansori* was also started long ago among the farmers and common people. In this special kind of drama, all the parts are spoken or sung by one person, accompanied only by a barrel drum. The performer must be able to change voice styles very quickly to portray the different characters. Sometimes the play lasts for several hours. Popular stories include the tale of a very smart rabbit who went into the sea to meet the King of the Oceans; the story of a poor but kind younger brother and his rich and mean older brother; and the story of a daughter who gave up her own life so that her blind father could see again.

Bamboo Orchestras

Korean people love music. They enjoy singing, dancing, and playing instruments. They like to listen to the kind of orchestra music played in North America and Europe—music played on violins, cellos, and French horns. But they especially like their own orchestra music.

Korean orchestra music is played on the *taegum*, *kayagum*, and *changgo*. The *taegum* (teh-goom) is a flute with thirteen holes. It is made of bamboo and has a clear, beautiful tone. The *kayagum* (ka-yah-goom) is a harp with twelve strings. It is

These young women are playing a kayagum, *a kind of harp.*

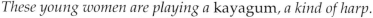

made of a lightweight wood. The *changgo* (chang-go) is a drum shaped like an hourglass. On one side, the drum skin is hit with the hand. On the other side, it is hit with a bamboo stick. These kinds of musical instruments were once used in performances for kings and noblemen.

When playing these and other Korean instruments, the musicians always sit on the floor. Even the singers sit on the floor. And the performers always wear brightly colored clothing—reds, blues, greens, and whites.

Brush and Ink

Imagine writing a word on a sheet of poster board with a marker and then watching people come by to admire it. That is what happens in Korea. People admire the way letters are shaped. Writing words so that the letters convey the feeling of the words is called calligraphy.

The writing can be as beautiful as a painting. In old Korea, someone who could write beautiful letters with a brush was

Long ago, people learned the art of beautiful writing in calligraphy schools. This classroom is part of a historic village, where people re-create life in old Korea.

KOREA IN ARTS AND LETTERS

Buddhist monks. In the year 1251, Buddhist monks finished making a complete set of Buddhist scriptures. They carved each page on wooden blocks—in reverse—so that the scriptures could be printed for people to read. Altogether, they carved more than 80,000 wood blocks. These blocks were destroyed by invaders, but a second set, made in the 1300s, is a Korean national treasure. It is stored in Haein-sa Temple in South Korea.

Chong Son* (1676–1759), painter. He is famous for painting beautiful Korean landscapes full of detail and life. In his day, many painters stayed inside their studios to paint. Chong Son said that painters should go out into the world and paint what they saw. One of his famous paintings is called *Clearing After the Rain on Inwang Mountain.*

Kim So-wol (1902–1943), poet. He was one of the first Korean poets who allowed his work to be influenced by foreign writers, such as those in Europe and other places. The poem "Azaleas" is probably his most famous.

Pak Kyong-ni (1926–   ), novelist. She is the author of a novel called *The Land.* The story takes place in Korea during the time the Japanese controlled the country. In 1996, Korean writers chose *The Land*, published in 1995, as the most outstanding modern Korean novel.

* The family name is given first in Korea, followed by the personal name.

highly respected; learning calligraphy required study and self-discipline. With paper, ink, a brush, and patient effort, you can learn to write the way Koreans—as well as Chinese and Japanese—have for thousands of years.

In addition to making beautiful letters, Koreans are famous for painting colorful pictures. Dragons, tigers, priests, farmers, homemakers, and soldiers are some favorite subjects. But perhaps the most beautiful paintings are of nature and the countryside: mountains, flowers, trees, butterflies, clouds. This landscape style of painting is similar to Chinese and Japanese landscape painting.

Inventions Galore!

There have been times in Korea's long history when its people have been especially creative. One of those times was between 500 and 600 years ago, during the Choson era. During this period, Koreans invented movable metal type. This invention made it much easier to print books. Before this time, books had to be copied by hand or printed from blocks of wood with the words and pictures carved in reverse. Another valuable invention, made in 1442, was the copper rain gauge. This instrument allowed farmers to know precisely how much rainwater had fallen on their fields.

Why were there so many inventions at this time? Part of the reason was that King Sejong (1418–1450) gathered many educated people together in one place, called the College of Scholars. The king provided the money for these scientists to spend their time inventing things. Scientists also wrote books on medicine and farming and created a new way of writing down musical notes. In addition, they studied the solar system in order to develop a better calendar.

Palaces and Temples

Koreans were famous not only for their useful inventions, but also for their large and beautiful palaces and temples. The foundations of these buildings were laid with stone. The walls were made of wood, and the roofs of heavy, clay tiles. Sometimes a statue of a fish or another creature was put on the top of the roof. The Koreans believed that the statue would protect the building from fire or other damage.

The rooms inside a palace were warm because the builders put heating vents under the wooden floors. Heat from the stove in the kitchen flowed through small tunnels

Korea's temples, such as this one with a huge statue of Buddha, are elaborate and beautiful.

under the floors. Elderly people were always allowed to sit directly on top of the heat tunnels, where it was warmest. This system of heating is still used in many Korean homes.

Walls inside homes, palaces, and temples were made of light wood. Sliding doors of paper and wood separated the rooms. On the floor were thin mats of straw. People would sit on the floor on cushions and sleep on the floor on mats.

A temple might have a statue inside. Usually, this would be a statue of Buddha or another religious figure. Korean artists made these statues from metal, stone, clay, and wood. Some of the statues were covered with a thin layer of sparkling gold, and some were painted with brilliant colors. Many were sculpted more than 1,000 years ago, but they are still standing. Today Koreans look at these statues and remember the teachings of their religions, or they simply admire the work of the artists.

These intricately carved wooden statues are painted in bright colors.

Of course, no palace or temple would be complete without a garden. Korean gardens are designed with many beautiful bushes and trees. They contain ponds or small lakes filled with colorful fish, swans, and ducks. Although the gardens have been created by people, they have been made to look as though they were natural. People like to walk through the gardens to enjoy nature or just to sit quietly in them and think.

More New Technology Ideas

Korean people of the past invented many things; Koreans today are still very creative. South Koreans make products that people buy all around the world, such as televisions and VCRs. They also make many of the memory chips inside computers. South Koreans, in fact, build more electronic products than all but five other countries in the world.

South Koreans also build many of the cars people drive and many of the ships that carry oil around the world. You may be wearing clothes that were made in South Korea.

Workers spin, weave, and dye the cloth using modern machines. Some of the clothing is made from cotton and wool bought from the United States, Australia, and China. Some is made from newly invented chemical threads.

The Korean peninsula has no oil under the ground. Both North and South Korea must buy their oil from other countries. But they have built modern factories where the oil is processed into gasoline for use in cars and trucks.

To communicate, Koreans (especially South Koreans) use regular and cellular telephones, fax machines, and electronic (computer) mail. Almost everyone watches television and listens to the radio. Many communication signals are beamed into space to a Korean satellite and then sent back down to earth. Some 80,000 scientists in South Korea alone are experimenting with new ways of making things that will help people. The ancient spirit of invention still thrives in modern Korea.

Samsung, a company that makes television sets, is one of many high-tech businesses in South Korea.

Country Facts

SOUTH KOREA

Official Name: Taehan Minguk (Republic of Korea; South Korea)

Capital: Seoul

Location: a peninsula projecting southward from northeast China. Its northern border is North Korea. Across the Sea of Japan is Japan, and across the Yellow Sea to the west is the People's Republic of China.

Area: 38,230 square miles (98,480 square kilometers). *Greatest distances:* east-west, 185 miles (298 kilometers); north-south, 300 miles (480 kilometers). *Coastline:* 1,499 miles (2,413 kilometers)

Elevation: *Highest:* Mount Hallasan, located on Cheju Island, 6,399 feet (1,950 meters). *Lowest:* sea level along the coast

Climate: dry, cold winters with storms from Siberia. Hot, humid, rainy summers. August is the wettest month of the year.

Population: 45,553,882 South Koreans (about 69 million North and South Koreans combined). *Distribution:* 79 percent urban; 21 percent rural. More than 4 million Koreans live abroad, in the United States, Japan, China, Russia, and other countries.

Form of Government: representative democracy that is headed by a president

Important Products: Fish. *Natural Resources:* coal, lead, tungsten, and hydropower. *Agriculture:* rice, barley, fruit, and vegetables. *Industries:* clothing, shoes, cars, shipbuilding, and electronics

Basic Unit of Money: won; 1 won = 100 chon

Language: Korean

Religion: Buddhism, Christianity, Confucianism, shamanism

Flag: blue and red yin/yang symbol in the center with a white background; black bars are in each corner. The flag is called the *Taegŭkki.*

National Anthem: *Aegug-ga* ("Love of Country")

Major Holidays: New Year's Day, January 1; Independence Movement Day, March 1; Arbor Day, April 5; Buddha's Birthday, varies (based on lunar calendar); Children's Day,

May 5; Memorial Day, June 6; Farmers' Day, June 15; Constitution Day, July 17; Liberation Day, August 15; Harvest Moon Festival, September or October (varies from year to year); Armed Forces Day, October 1; National Foundation Day, October 3; National Language Day, October (varies from year to year); Christmas, December 25

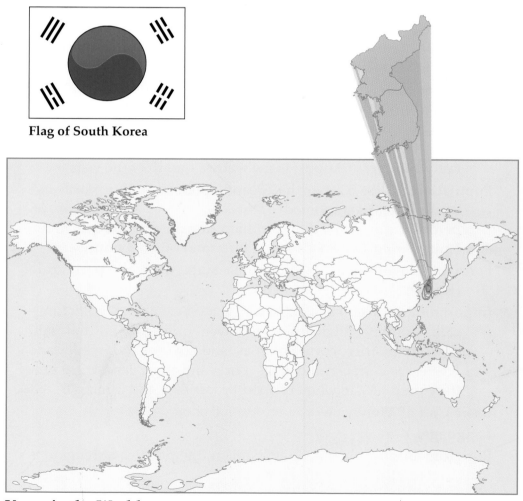

Flag of South Korea

Korea in the World

Country Facts

NORTH KOREA

Official Name: Choson Minjujuui Inmin Konghwaguk (Democratic People's Republic of Korea). *Choson* means "land of the morning calm"

Capital: Pyongyang

Location: a peninsula projecting southward from northeast China. It shares its northern border with Russia and China and its southern border with South Korea. Across the Sea of Japan is Japan, and across the Yellow Sea to the west is the People's Republic of China.

Area: 46,541 square miles (120,540 square kilometers). *Greatest distances:* east-west, 320 miles (515 kilometers); north-south, 370 miles (595 kilometers). *Coastline:* 665 miles (1,070 kilometers)

Elevation: *Highest:* Mount Paektusan, located on the northern border with China, 9,003 feet (2,744 meters). *Lowest:* sea level along the coast

Climate: dry, cold winters with storms from Siberia. Hot, humid, rainy summers. August is the wettest month of the year.

Population: 23,486,550 North Koreans (about 69 million North and South Koreans combined). *Distribution:* 64 percent urban; 36 percent rural. More than 4 million Koreans live abroad, in the United States, Japan, Russia, China, and other countries.

Form of Government: Communist state with one-party rule (Korean Workers' Party)

Important Products: Fish. *Natural Resources:* coal, lead, gold, tungsten, graphite, hydroelectric power, iron, copper, and salt. *Agriculture:* rice, corn, potatoes, and soybeans. *Livestock and livestock products:* cattle, hogs, pork, and eggs. *Industries:* military products, machinery, food processing, and mining

Basic Unit of Money: won; 1 won = 100 chon

Language: Korean

Religion: Buddhism and Confucianism (the practice of religion is discouraged by the government)

Flag: two narrow blue bars on the top and bottom, separated by white stripes from a large red field. In the red field is an off-center white circle with a red star in it

National Anthem: "The Song of General Kim Il-Sung"

Major Holidays: New Year's Day, January 1; Kim Jong Il's Birthday, February 16; International Women's Day, March 8; Kim Il-Sung's Birthday, April 15; May Day, May 1; National Liberation Day, August 15; National Foundation Day, September 9; National Language Day, October (varies from year to year); Anniversary of the Foundation of the Korean Workers' Party, October 10; Anniversary of the Constitution, December 27.

Flag of North Korea

Glossary

Buddhism: a religion, followed mainly in central and east Asia, that teaches that people can overcome suffering through mental discipline. It was founded about 2,500 years ago by a man named Siddhartha Gautama, who became known as the Buddha, or the Enlightened One.

calligraphy: the art of writing letters with beautiful penmanship

capitalism: a type of economy in which people and companies can own private property and can buy and sell products without government control

celadon pottery: a famous Korean ceramics style, usually light blue-green in color

communism: a type of government in which a single political party controls or owns all the land and the businesses and issues strict rules about all aspects of social and economic life

Confucianism: the philosophy of the Chinese thinker Confucius. This philosophy holds that society would be in harmony if people followed the rules of the positions of life into which they were born.

dictatorship: a type of government in which a single person or a small group of people have almost complete authority

dynasty: a powerful family that rules a country generation after generation

genealogy: a record of one's ancestors

hanbok: a kind of traditional clothing that is worn on special occasions

juche (joo-cheh): a Korean word for self-reliance. The word signifies the philosophy of former North Korean leader Kim Il-Sung.

lacquer: coating for boxes, furniture, and other objects in which layers of rice glue, charcoal powder, and a clear varnish are applied and then polished to make a smooth, shiny surface

missionary: a person who is sent by his or her religious group to spread that religion to others

Mongolia: a country north of China. The Mongols ruled China and Korea for many years.

peninsula: a body of land almost entirely surrounded by water but connected to the mainland

shamanism: a religion whose followers believe in an unseen world of spirits—gods, demons, and ancestor spirits—that can be influenced by shamans, or priests

sseajok (sea-joke): clan; the members of an extended family

won (wan): money; Korean currency

For Further Reading

Bandon, Alexandra. *Korean Americans.* Englewood Cliffs, New Jersey: Silver Burdett, 1994.

Clay, Rebecca. *Our Human Family: Ties That Bind.* Woodbridge, Connecticut: Blackbirch Press, 1996.

Dubois, Jill. *South Korea.* Tarrytown, New York: Marshall Cavendish, 1993.

Farley, Carol. *Korea: Land of the Morning Calm.* Englewood Cliffs, New Jersey: Silver Burdett, 1991.

Loewen. *Food in Korea.* Vero Beach, Florida: The Rourke Corporation, 1991.

McNair, Sylvia. *Korea.* Chicago: Childrens Press, 1989.

Nash, Amy K. *North Korea.* New York: Chelsea House, 1991.

Solberg, S. E. *The Land and People of Korea.* New York: HarperCollins Children's Books, 1991.

Index

Page numbers for illustrations are in boldface

animism, 21. *See also* shamanism
architecture, 52–53, **53**
arts, **46**, 47–54

Buddhism, 22, 23, **35**
Buddhist monks, 48, 51
bulgogi, 37, **38**
businesses, **16**, 23, **26**

calligraphy, 50–51
calligraphy school, 50, **50**
celadon pottery, **46**, 47–48
changgo, 49, 50
Chinese customs, 12, 14
Choson era, 13, 52
Chyongmyo T'aeje Temple, 34
climate, 11
clothing, 27, **27**, **32**, 33, 34, 36
Confucianism, 20, 21, 22, 23
Confucian monks, **28**, 34
Confucius, 20, 21, 22, 31
Confucius class system, 20–21
crops, 11, **11**, 25

education, 20, 21, **21**, 27, 41–43, **43**

family history, 32–33
family life, 29–34, 38
farming, 11, 24, **24**, 25
and irrigation, 10
festivals, **28**, 33–34
food, 33, 36–39, **38**, **39**

games, 33, 43–44
geography, 8–11
government, 15, 18, 19, 23, 26, 33

Heaven, Lake of, 10
history, 11–15
holidays, 19, 33–36, **36**
homes, 31

inventions, 52

Japan, Sea of, 8, 10

kayagum, 49–50, **50**
kimchi, 37, **38**
kingdoms
    Koguryo, 12
    Paekche, 12
    Silla, 12
Korea Strait, 9
Korean War, 14–15
Koryo dynasty, 12
Kwangju, **6**

language, 14, 18–19, 35

masked dancers, 48, **48**
Mongolia, 12, 17
Mountain of Eternal Snow, 8. *See also* Paektusan
mountains, of Korea, 8–10
music, 49–50

North Korea
    creation of, 14
    education in, 42, 43
    government of, 15, 23, 26, 32
    holidays, 34–35
    language of, 18, 19
    military, 26
    money and, 23
    name of, 14, 15
    religion in, 22
    villages, 24
    workers in, 24, 25

paddies, 11, **11**
Paektusan, 7, 8, 10
pansori, 48–49
pavilions, **6**
peoples, of Korea, 12, 17–27
    elderly, 31, **31**, 38, 53
population, 18
Pyongyang, 25

religion, 21–23, **35**
rivers, of Korea, 10–11

Samsung, 24, **55**
Sejong, 18, 52
Seoul, 13, **13**, 16, 25, **25**, 34, 36, 39, **39**, 45
shaman, 21–22
shamanism, 22, **22**
Soraksan National Park, **9**
South Korea
    businesses, **16**, **55**
    cities, **6**, 24
    creation of, 14
    education in, 27, 42–43, **43**
    government of, 15, 23, 26
    holidays, 34–35, **36**
    language of, 18–19
    military, 26
    money and, 23
    name of, 14
    religion in, 22, 23, **35**
    workers in, 24–26, 54–55
sports, **40**, 44, 45, **45**
statues, 53, **53**, **54**
Sunjong, 14

Taedong River, 10
taegum, 49
taekwondo, 45, **45**
Tangun, legend of, 7–8
technology, 54–55
Toson Temple, **36**
Tumen River, 10
turtle ships, 13–14

weddings, 27, 32
won, 33

Yalu River, 10
Yellow Sea, 8, 10
Yi dynasty, 13, 34
Yi Song-gye, 13
Yi Sun-sin, 13

About the Author

Dean W. Collinwood is Professor of Sociology and Director of Asian Studies at Weber State University and Adjunct Professor at the University of Utah. He has degrees from the University of Chicago, the University of London, and Brigham Young University. He currently directs the Utah Asian Studies Consortium (UCON) and the U.S.-Japan Center of Utah and is a member of the boards of the Japan-America Society of Utah, the Utah Academy of Sciences, Arts, and Letters, and the Western Conference of the Association for Asian Studies. He is the author of *Global Studies: Japan and the Pacific Rim* and other books and articles on Asia. He and his wife, Kathleen, and their children live near Salt Lake City, Utah.